I AM SOULSHINE

"Don't you know yet?
It is your light that lights the worlds."

. . . Rumi

I AM SOULSHINE

Tiffany Ehnes

Argosian
PUBLISHING
Advance, NC USA

Argosian Publishing
429 Rainbow Rd., Advance, NC 27006 USA
www.argosian.com

Published in the United States of America

I AM SOULSHINE
Copyright@Tiffany Ehnes, 2015
All rights reserved

ISBN 978-1-7340522-6-8
Printed, 2021

Library of Congress Control Number: 2021938337

The text of this book was typeset in Lightfoot.
Accent text was typeset in Soleil.

Rumi quote is public domain.
Photographs copyright@the respective photographer information found
in Photography Credits located at the end of the book.

Argosian
PUBLISHING

With empowering words and awe-inspiring photography, this book helps guide you gently through your inner chakra system. Chakras are the energy centers within the body that are described in the ancient Sanskrit and the Old Testament. They play an important role in our mental, physical, emotional, and spiritual well-being

Follow along as each beautiful page within this book assists you in healing and balancing your energy. As we bring our chakra system back into alignment, we allow the most vibrant and radiant version of ourselves to shine through.

●	**Violet**	Spirituality, Wisdom, Inspiration
●	**Indigo**	Self Realization, Intuition, Imagination
●	**Blue**	Self Expression, Communication, Trust
●	**Green**	Self Love, Compassion, Relationships
●	**Yellow**	Self Esteem, Confidence, Knowledge
●	**Orange**	Emotions, Confidence, Creativity
●	**Red**	Roots, Family, Grounding

I AM ROOTED

I AM EXPLORING MY WORLD

I AM NATURE

I AM IN A COMMUNITY

I AM A FRIEND

I AM JOYFUL

I AM CELEBRATING EVERYTHING

I AM CHANGING THE WORLD

I AM PLAYFUL

I AM
EXPANDING

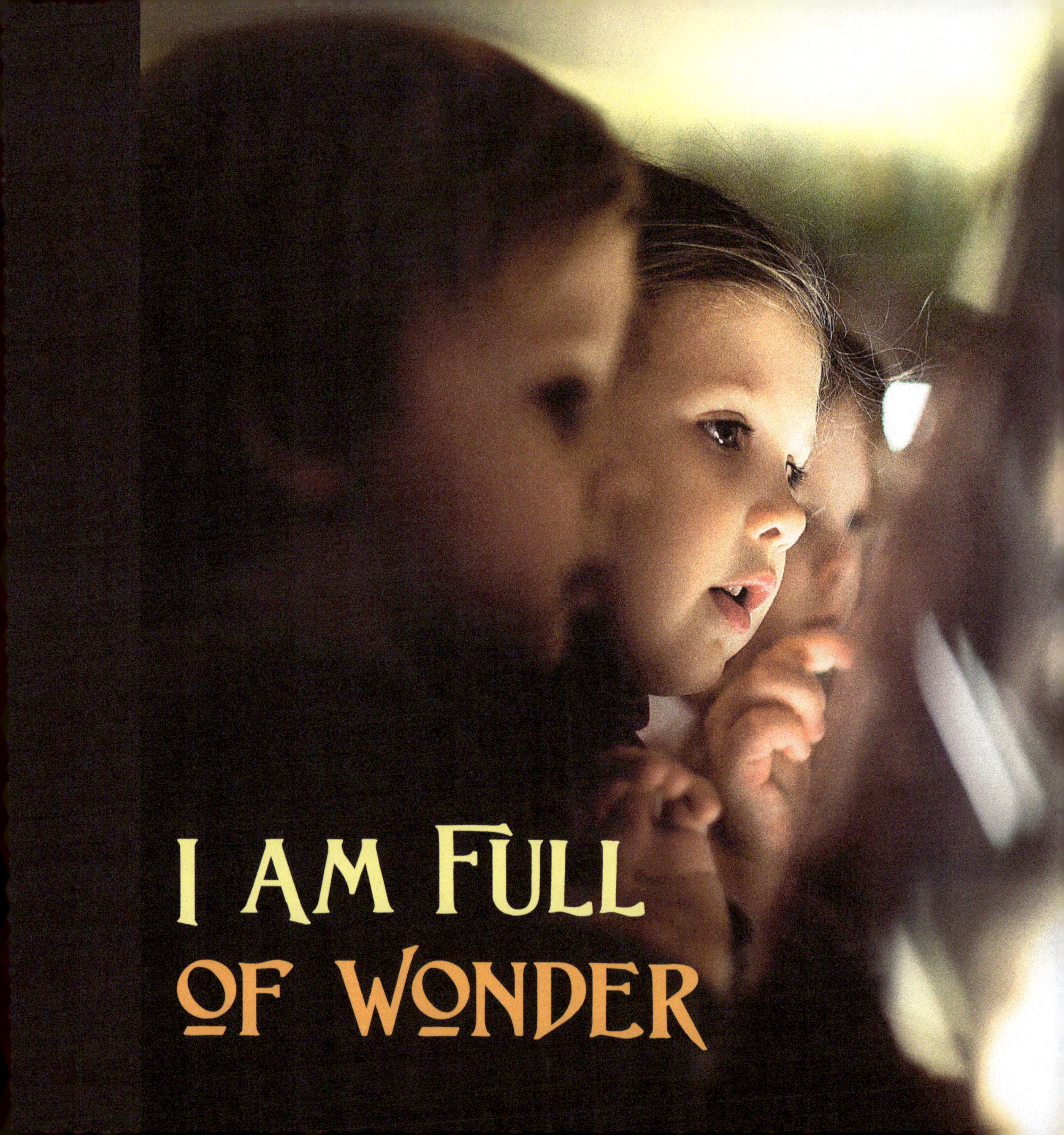
I AM FULL
OF WONDER

I AM STRONG
. . . INSIDE

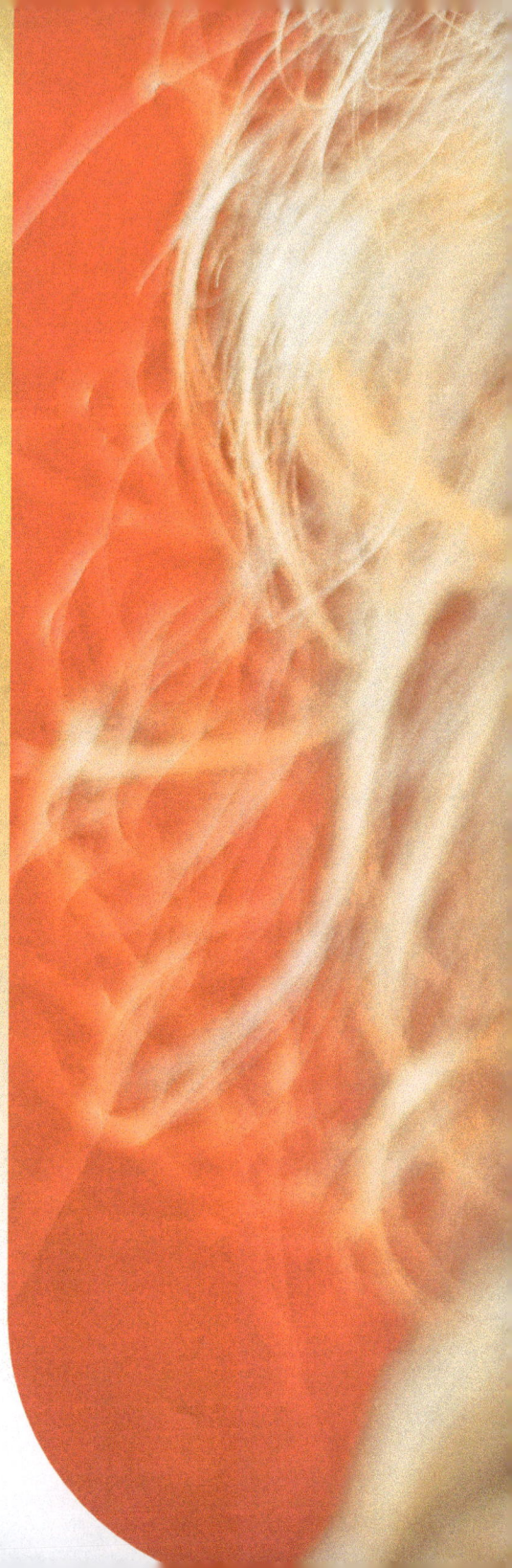

I AM TRANSCENDING BOUNDARIES

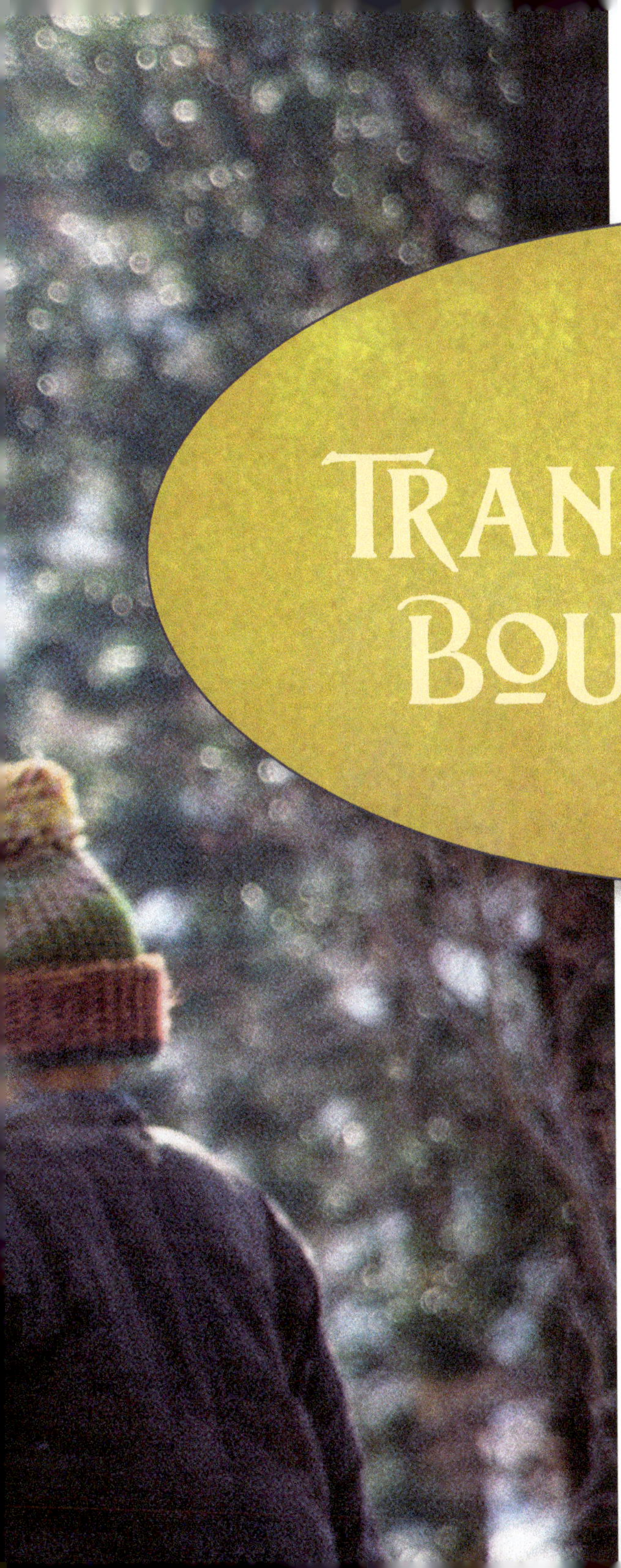

I AM MOVING AT THE SPEED OF CHANGE

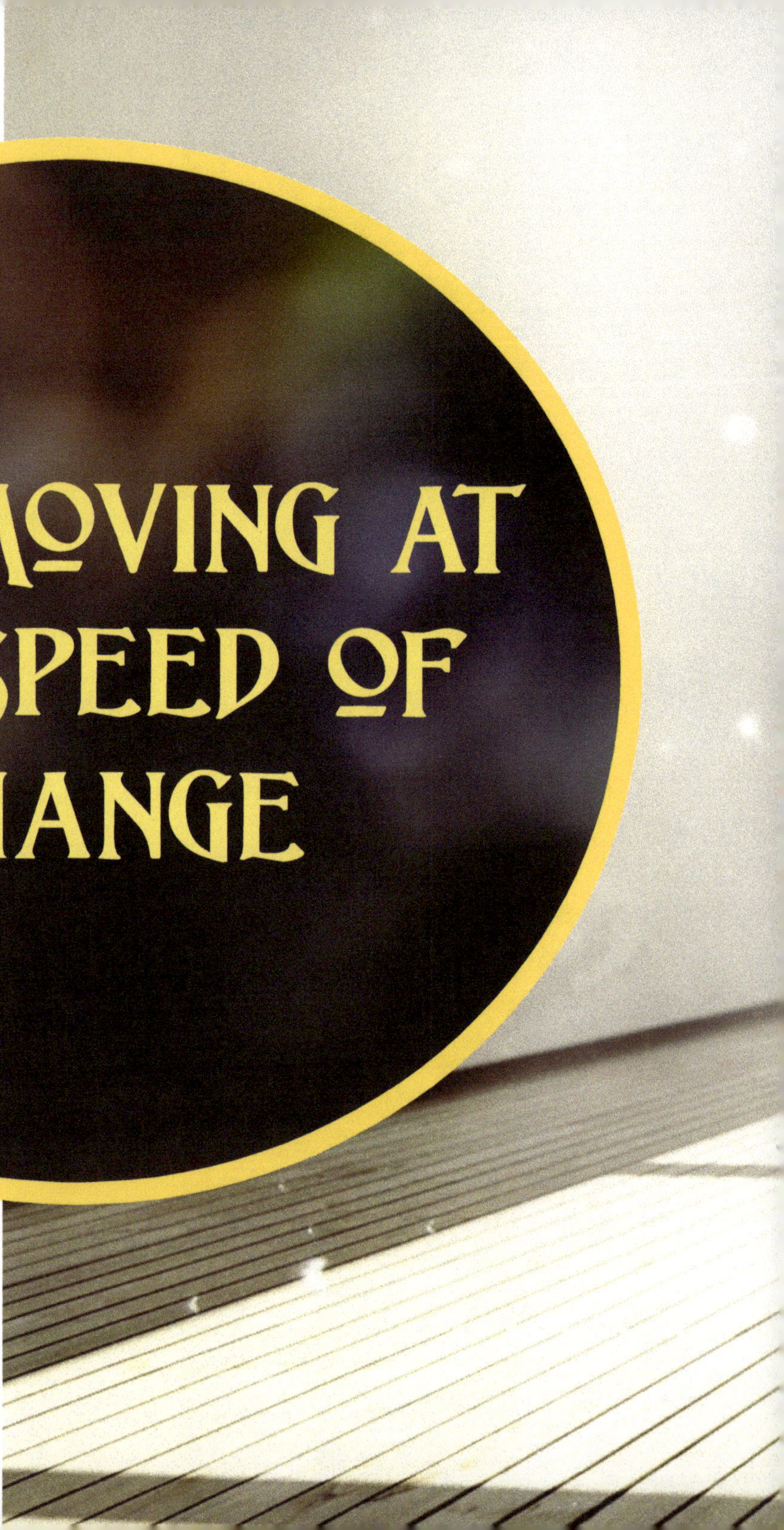

I AM FABULOUS

I AM DEEPLY LOVED

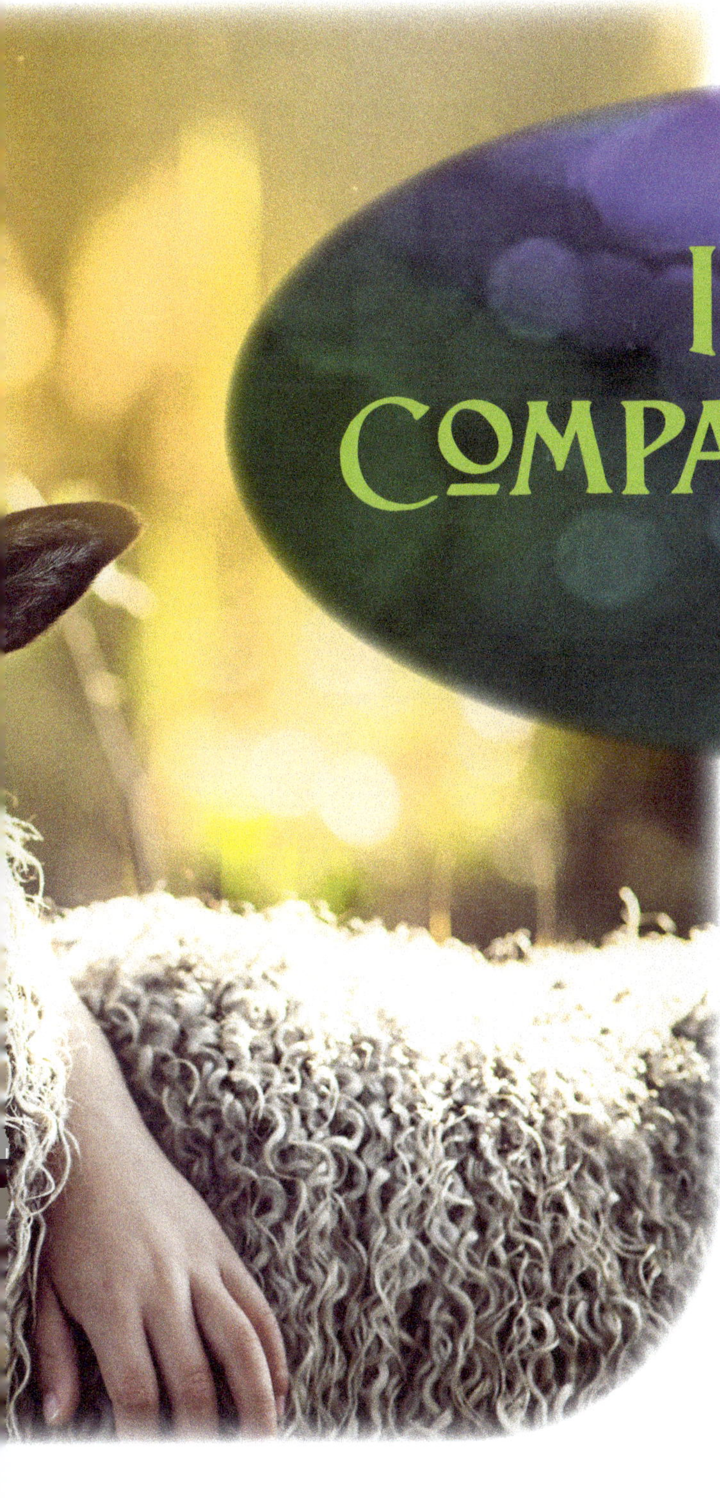

I Am Compassionate

I AM PRACTICING KINDNESS

I AM FORGIVING

I AM
PEACE

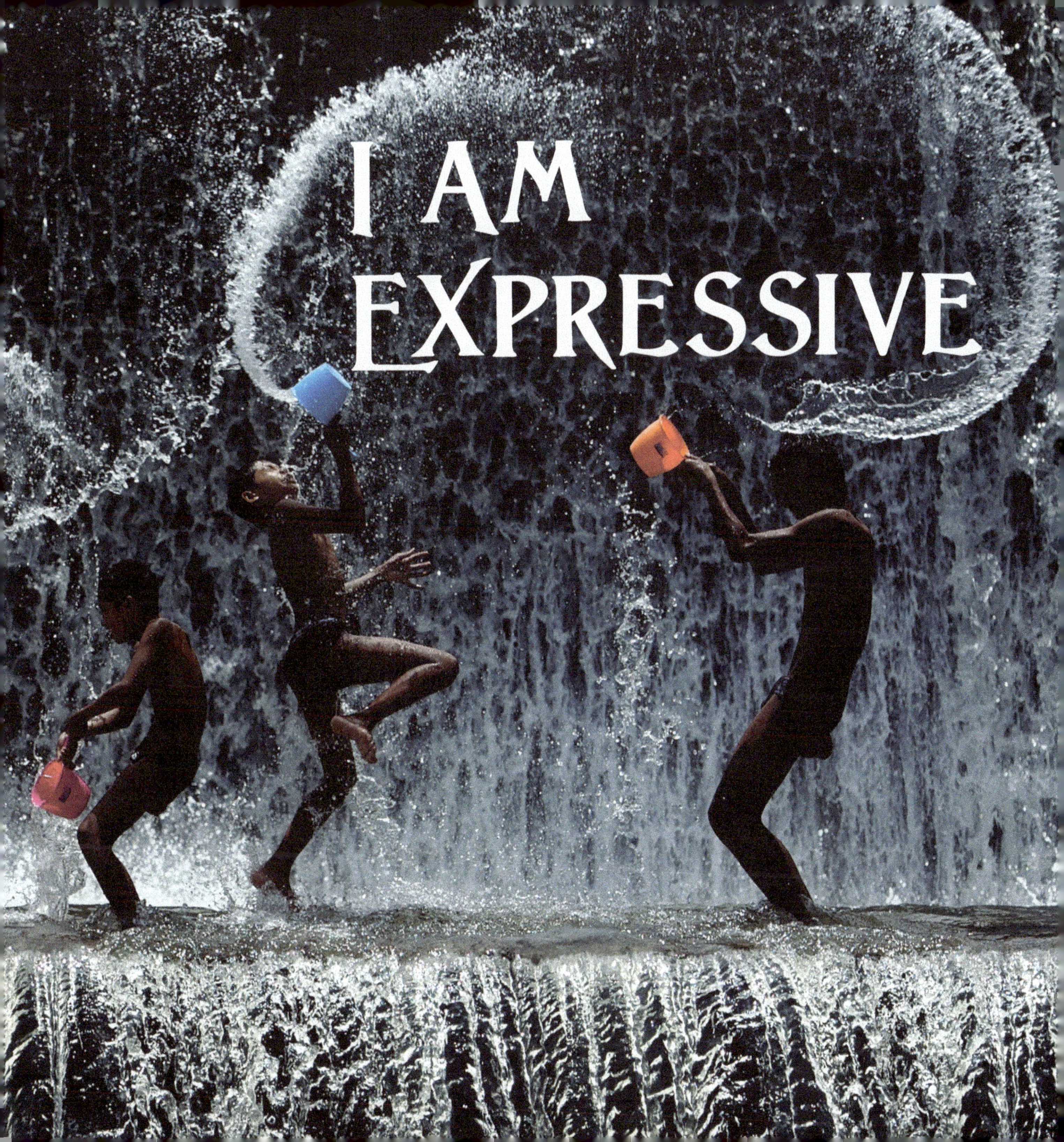
I AM
EXPRESSIVE

I AM SPEAKING
MY TRUTH

I AM
INSPIRED

I AM
LISTENING

I AM ALIVE

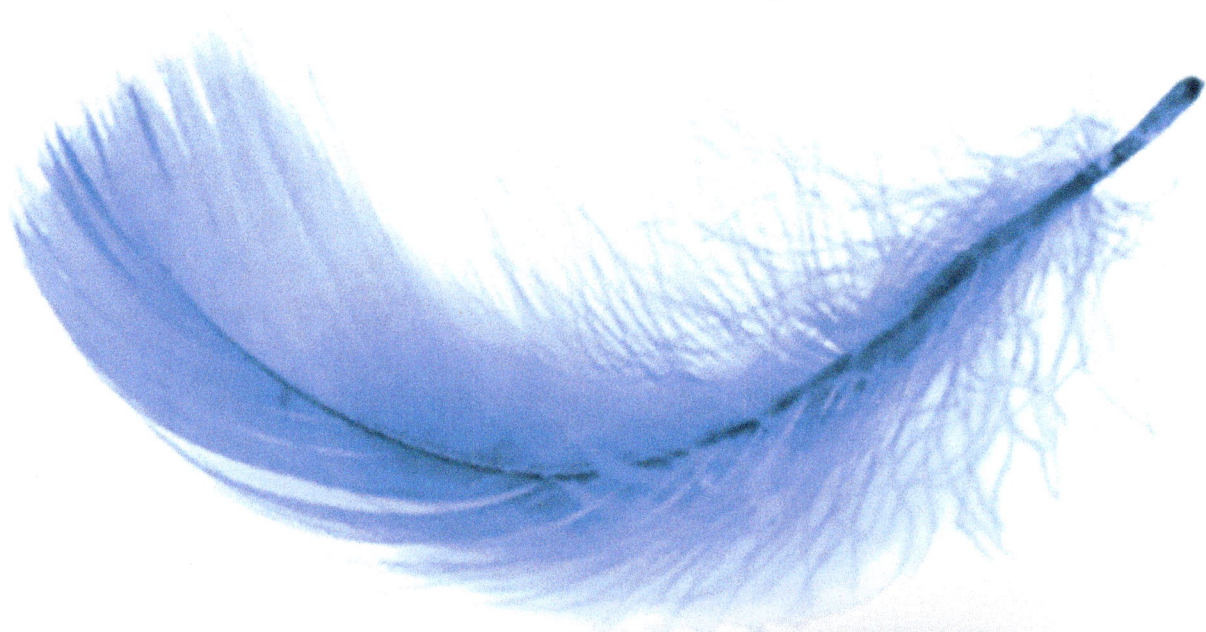

I AM
CONNECTED

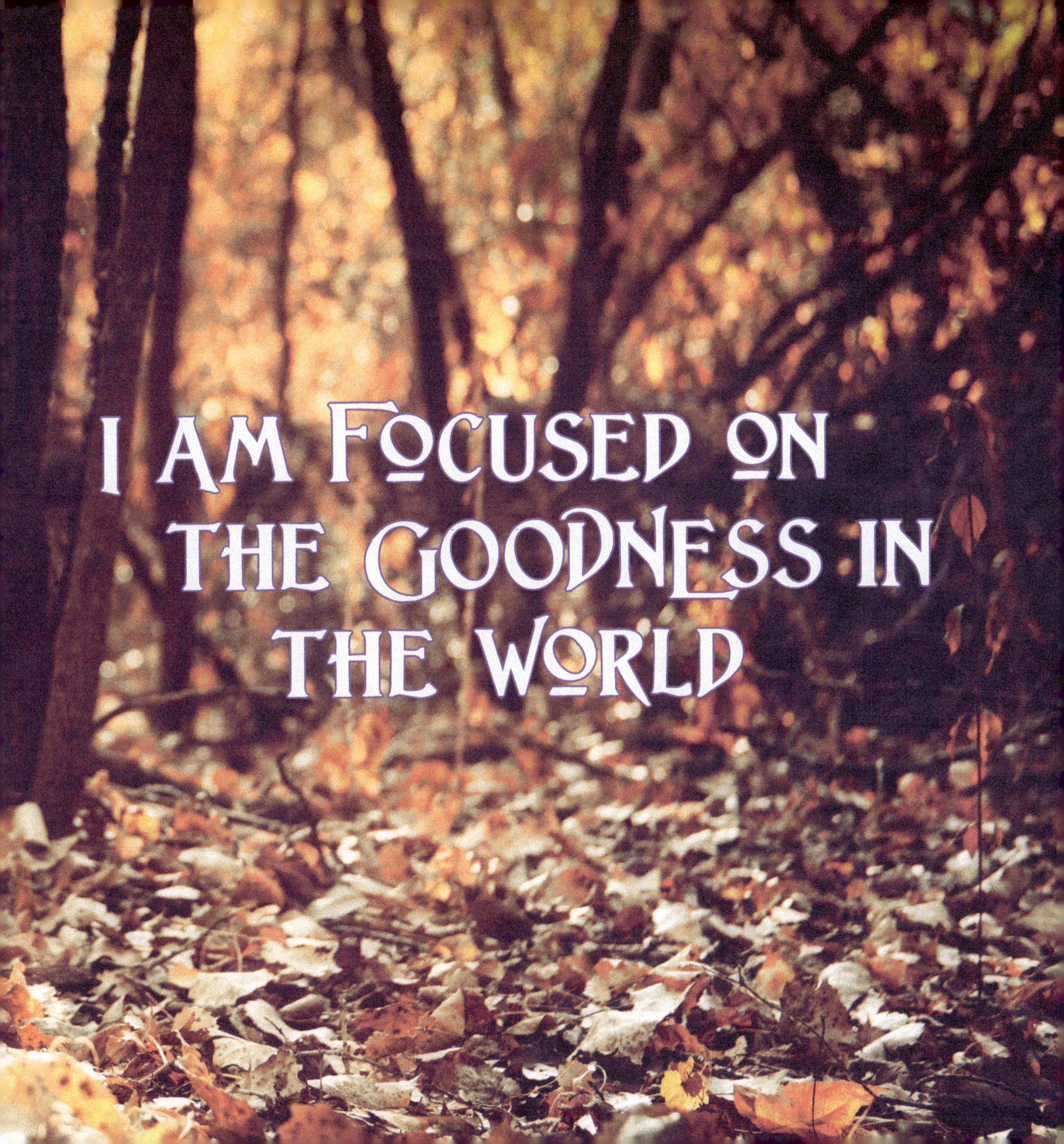
I AM FOCUSED ON
THE GOODNESS IN
THE WORLD

I AM
REMEMBERING
WHO I AM

I AM HERE FOR A SPECIAL REASON

I AM FULL OF IMAGINATION

I AM DIVINE

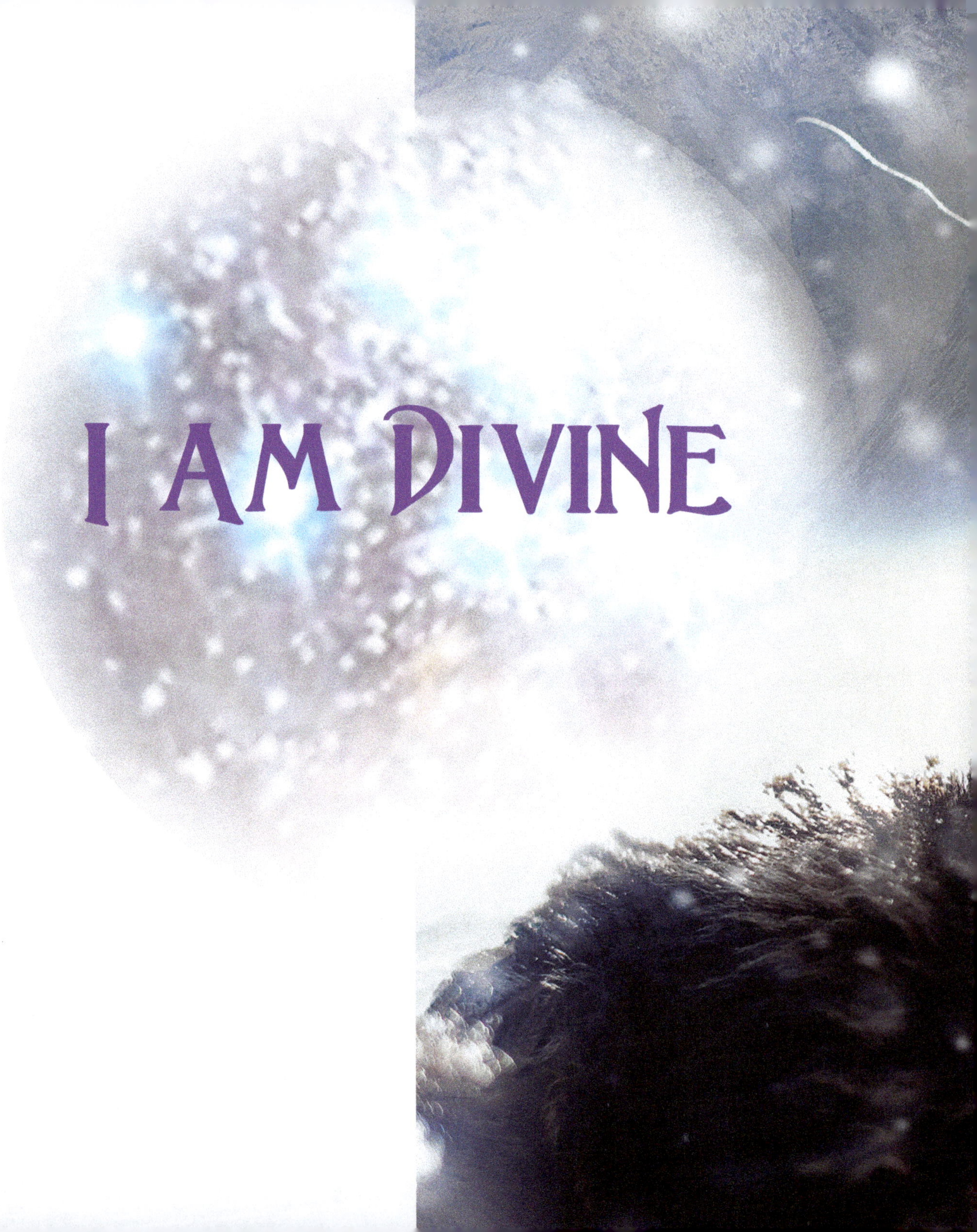

I AM
INFINITE ENERGY

I AM CREATED BY THE SOURCE THAT CREATES GALAXIES

I AM WORTHY

I AM FREE TO BE ME & I AM AMAZING

PHOTOGRAPHY CREDITS

Photographers (Listed Alphabetically) I would like to thank and recognize these award-winning photographers whose amazing work aligned with my vision.

Amandine Adrien is a passionate Parisian photographer specializing in portrait and fashion photography. She prefers photos which tell stories and convey emotions. http://amandine-adrien.com
- I am exploring my world: Little Princess – France

Michal Bednarek is a creative professional photographer from Poland, who specializes in commercial and artistic photography. http://photocreo.com
- I am here for a special reason: Maasai School Children – Ngorongoro, Tanzania

Hardijanto Budiman (Habe) is a self-taught photographer and artist from Jakarta, Indonesia. He enjoys drawing, painting, and expressing his passion through photography. www.habegraphy.com or hardibudi.1x.com
- I am playful: The Race – Jakarta, Indonesia

JP Hallet © All Rights Reserved: S. Fassberg, Connectingdotz.com. Jean-Pierre Hallet was a Belgian adventurer, naturalist, humanitarian and art collector who became a blood brother of the Lega, Tutsi and Nande tribes, and was initiated as a Massai warrior. www.Connectingdotz.com
- I am connected: Osani Circle Game – Republic of Congo, Central Africa. Efé children of the Ituri Forest in Zaire begin the Osani game sitting in a circle, all connected.

Elika Hunt is a wedding and portrait photographer, based in Estonia. She draws her inspiration from fine art photography, music, dance, nature and her family. www.elikahunt.com
- I am created by the source that creates galaxies: Girl in Pink – Estonia

Sarawut Intarob is a photographer from Bangkok, Thailand and photography manager at HACK Gallery. www.facebook.com/Srw.hack
- I am practicing kindness: Smile – Camtakra District, Sakonnakon, Thailand
- I am peace: Happy Time – Kosumpisai District, Bungkan, Thailand
- I am worthy: Tibetan Bo – Xigaze District, Tibet

I Gede Lila Kantiana is a professional Balinese photographer for wedding, commercial, architecture, and fashion photography. He won numerous awards for his work which specializes in the "human interest." www.lilaartphoto.com
- I am deeply loved: Cheers When Rain Arrives – Bogor, Indonesia
- I am infinite energy: Go...Go...Go...!! – Bogor, Indonesia

Alexia Khruscheva is an award-winning Russia photographer specializing in equestrian photos. www.photolex.net
- I am a friend: Child Feeding Pony & Horse Running in Winter Forest – Russia

Viola Krupova is a Slovak architect and photographer currently living in Qatar. Her photographical work is represented by digitally modified photos combined in such a way that they mimic old, traditional paintings. www.mvimaginarium.sk
  • I am celebrating everything: Henryk Wieniawski: Gypsy Melodies – Slovak

Svetlana Kvashina is an award-winning Russian photographer whose creativity was inspired by the birth of her daughter in 2010. She specializes in photos that tell stories and come alive through light and emotion. http://kvashina.35photo.ru or https://500px.com/SvetlanaKvashina
  • I am expanding: Sun Catcher – Russia
  • I am fabulous: Boy & Cat Fishing
  • I am speaking my truth: Wonder
  • I am inspired: Winter Draws...

Rodrigo Lanzillotta is a freelance photographer from Buenos Aires, Argentina who specializes in sporting and social events, weddings, communions, advertising and fashion. He is the conceptual designer of this photograph. www.facebook.com/pages/Lanzillotta-Studio or http://rodylanz.wix.com/lanzillottastudio
  • I am moving at the speed of change: Ballerina – Buenos Aires, Argentina

David Lazar is a travel photographer and musician from Brisbane, Australia, who captures moments of life, beauty and culture in his photography. David's portraits and landscapes have been published in National Geographic, Lonely Planet, in-flight, travel and photography magazines and he has won numerous awards. www.davidlazarphoto.com
  • I am rooted: The Tree of Life – Burma; A novice monk sits on the roots of an ancient tree. Buddhism is based upon love, tolerance and compassion.
  • I am in a community: Seven Monks on a Log – Yangon, Myanmar; Novice monks grow up together in their monastery, forming a brotherhood.
  • I am Forgiving: Boy at Temple – Puthia, Bangladesh

Maria Moroz is a professional photographer from Saint Petersburg, Russia. http://us.fotolia.com
  • Cover & I am divine: The Winter's Tale – Russia

Jake Olson is an award-winning, professional photographer from Blair, Nebraska. Jake Olson Studios has also been featured on The Weather Channel and in dozens of publications around the world including British Vogue and Digital SLR Magazine. www.jakeolsonstudios.com
  • Inside page & I am full of imagination: Glow – Nebraska, USA
  • I am joyful: Pixie
  • I am changing the world: In Dreams
  • I am remembering who I am: Self-Reflection
  • I am focused on the goodness in the world: Girl in Leaves

Anna Karin Palsson is a professional photographer from Sweden. She is passionate about photography and digital art. 500px.com/AnnaKarinPlsson or www.facebook.com/fotografannakarinpalsson
  • I am compassionate: Hi There Little Friend – Sweden

Mary Roux is a professional photographer from Rome, New York and the owner of Portrait Pizzaz. www.portraitpizzaz.com
  • I am nature: Tree Art – Rome, New York, USA

Hamid Sardar-Afkhami has a Ph.D. from Harvard University. He is a documentary film maker and photographer living in France. Inspired by the pioneers of exploration photography, he devotes his cameras to telling the story of endangered cultures who maintain a spiritual dialogue with the natural world. His work has been featured in prestigious publications such as National Geographic, Geo, Le Figaro Magazine and Paris Match. http://hamidsardarphoto.com
  • I am transcending boundaries: Reindeer Girls – Tsaatan (Dukha) Reindeer Nomads

Alex Goh Chun Seong is a freelance photographer based in the sunny island of Penang, Malaysia. For Alex, photography is his artistic expression with every shot captured spinning its own tale. https://500px.com/AlexGcs
  • I am expressive: Splashing Fun Time – Tukad Unda Dam, Bali

Elena Shumilova is an award-winning photographer from Moscow, Russia. She uses all sorts of light conditions that give visual and emotional depth to the images. Her enchanting work of children and animals has been featured in numerous publications around the world. http://elenashumilova.smugmug.com
  • I am full of wonder: In the Bakery – Moscow, Russia

WestEnd61 is based in Munich, Germany and represents over 300 freelance European photographers with unusual imagery and contemporary photographs. www.facebook.com/westend61images
  • I am free to be me and I am amazing: Boy in Winter (Junge im Winter) – Germany

Natalya Zhukova is a successful Russian children's photographer and mother of five sons. She has won numerous awards including the title of "Best Photographer of the Year 2013." http://natashazhukova.com/
  • I am listening: Heat of My Breath – Russia

Stock Photographer from 123rf.com. The boy dancing is a Sioux Indian from the San Manuel Band at an Indian Pow Wow.
  • I am alive: Sioux Indian Boy – San Bernadino, California

Stock Photographer from Shutterstock.com
  • I am strong . . . inside: Caucasian Girl

Spot Photography
Anyka (Belgium)
Nednapa Chumjumpa (Thailand)
Pavel Konovalov (Russia)
Samart Boonyang (Thailand)

Graphic Designer
Art Outside the Box – Susanne Valla is a graphic designer and illustrator. www.facebook.com/susanneAOB

Creative Input
I would like to offer a special thank you to my husband and partner for his creative input, his diligence, and for his enduring understanding when my projects take over the dining room table in the quest to find "just the right photo" for this book.

Author
Tiffany Ehnes

Tiffany Ehnes is an award-winning professional writer and internationally published author with over 20 years of experience. Her books are available in over 195 countries through most major bookstores and her website www.tiffanyehnes.com.

Tiffany is the author of several books, including the children's books "Legend of the Spirit Bear," and "The Dog That Barked Bear." She is an educator and public speaker with a background in psychology, philosophy, history, and the humanities. The Coca-Cola Scholars Foundation honored Tiffany for her work in education.

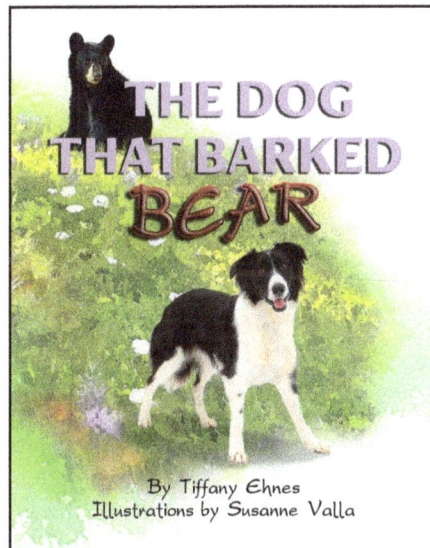

www.ingramcontent.com/pod-product-compliance
Lightning Source LLC
Chambersburg PA
CBHW040247100426
42811CB00011B/1178